Positive Affirmations for Black Women:
Success & Abundance Affirmations

Manifest Wealth, Money, Prosperity and Growth Mindset, Attract Business, and Financial Freedom, Overcome Imposter Syndrome

Tamara Jackson

Copyright 2025 – All rights reserved.

The content contained within this book may not be reproduced, duplicated or transmitted without direct written permission from the author or the publisher.

Under no circumstances will any blame or legal responsibility be held against the publisher, or author, for any damages, reparation, or monetary loss due to the information contained within this book. Either directly or indirectly.

Legal Notice:

This book is copyright protected.
This book is only for personal use. You cannot amend, distribute, sell, use, quote or paraphrase any part, or content within this book, without the consent of the author or publisher.

Disclaimer Notice:

Please not the information contained within this document is for educational and entertainment purposes only.

No warranties of any kind are declared or implied. Readers acknowledge that the author is not engaging in the rendering of legal, financial, medical or professional advice.

The content within this book has been derived from various sources. Please consult a licensed professional before attempting any techniques outlined in this book.

By reading this document, the reader agrees that under no circumstances is the author responsible for any losses, direct or indirect, which are incurred as a result of the use of the information contained within this document, including, but not limited to: errors, omissions, or inaccuracies.

Table of contents

Introduction 4
Part 1: Wealth, Growth, and Prosperity Mindset 6
Part 2: Attracting Opportunities and Financial Freedom .. 26
Part 3: Overcoming Imposter Syndrome 46
Part 4: Staying Focused on Goals 66
Part 5: Entrepreneurial Success Affirmations 86

Introduction

The Power of Your Mind and Words

Never underestimate the power of your mind and your words. Your thoughts shape your world, your confidence, and your destiny. Every idea you hold in your heart, every belief you repeat to yourself, lays the foundation for the reality you experience. As black women, we carry generations of resilience, beauty, and brilliance within us.

Your mind is your most powerful tool. When you feed it doubt, insecurity, and fear, those thoughts can take root and weigh you down. But when you **nurture it with strength, affirmation, and self-love, you awaken the unstoppable force within you.** You are not meant to second-guess your greatness. You are meant to **walk in it, stand tall in it, and let it radiate through every part of your being.**

This book is here to remind you of that power.

The Magic of Affirmations

Affirmations are declarations of truth, reminders of the queen that you are. When spoken with conviction, they shift your mindset, rewire your thoughts, and elevate your confidence. They allow you to take control of the narrative you tell yourself every day.

Imagine replacing the self-doubt and negative thoughts that try to creep in with words that uplift, affirm, and strengthen you. Imagine waking up each morning and declaring:

- *I am worthy of love, success, and joy.*
- *I am a Black woman, bold, brilliant, and unstoppable.*
- *My beauty, my mind, my energy – everything about me is divine.*

When you **speak life into yourself,** your energy shifts. You begin to embody the confidence, grace, and power that have always been within you. Your mind starts to believe the words you say, and before you know it, your actions align with your newfound confidence.

How to Use This Book

I encourage you to **read these affirmations aloud and own their power.** Feel their truth in your spirit. Say them in the mirror, write them in your journal, whisper them as you start your day, or repeat them as you drift off to sleep. **Let these affirmations become second nature, a part of your daily rhythm.**

The more you say them, the more they become **your truth.** You are reshaping your mindset, strengthening your self-love, and embracing your power with each repetition.

This journey is yours to take, and I am honored to walk beside you in it. **You are worthy. You are powerful. You are enough.**

Now, let's begin.

Part 1: Wealth, Growth, and Prosperity Mindset

I am worthy of wealth, success, and financial freedom.

Abundance flows to me effortlessly and consistently.

I am open to receiving unlimited prosperity.

My mind is a magnet for financial growth and success.

Every day, I attract new opportunities for wealth and expansion.

I am financially empowered and make wise money decisions.

My mindset is rooted in abundance, not scarcity.

Wealth is my birthright, and I claim it with confidence.

My actions align with my financial goals, leading me to prosperity.

I welcome financial success into my life with gratitude.

Money flows to me easily, freely, and abundantly.

I am a powerful creator of my own financial destiny.

I deserve all the wealth and success that comes my way.

I release all limiting beliefs about money and welcome prosperity.

Every dollar I spend and receive brings me joy and abundance.

I trust that the universe is always providing for me.

My income is constantly increasing, and I welcome the flow.

I attract wealth because I think abundantly and act with intention.

I am financially independent and secure in my success.

My wealth is a tool for creating positive change in my life and others.

I am grateful for the financial blessings that surround me.

Prosperity is drawn to me because I am open to receiving.

Every opportunity I take leads me to financial abundance.

I am always in the right place at the right time for wealth creation.

Success and prosperity are natural parts of my life.

I am confident in my ability to create and sustain wealth.

I deserve to be paid abundantly for my skills and talents.

I attract lucrative opportunities that align with my values.

I make money work for me and multiply my wealth effortlessly.

I release any fear or guilt associated with having wealth.

My financial future is bright, stable, and overflowing with abundance.

I embrace a millionaire mindset and take action accordingly.

I use my wealth to uplift myself, my family, and my community.

I am capable of achieving financial success beyond my wildest dreams.

Money is simply energy, and I welcome it with love and gratitude.

I take inspired action to increase my wealth and create lasting prosperity.

I am financially free, and I enjoy the security it brings.

I am deserving of financial abundance, and I allow it into my life.

The universe is constantly guiding me towards financial success.

I am financially savvy and make smart money choices.

I love seeing my bank account grow as I create more wealth.

My mind is focused on prosperity, and my reality reflects it.

My dreams are valid, and I have everything I need to achieve them.

I release all money blocks and welcome unlimited financial success.

I am always connected to new opportunities for financial growth.

I am fearless in my pursuit of financial success.

My financial blessings continue to grow, and I am grateful.

I confidently ask for and receive the financial abundance I deserve.

I am rich in every sense—wealth, love, knowledge, and opportunity.

I am a wealth magnet, and my prosperity is limitless.

I live in a world of abundance, and I claim my share of prosperity.

I create financial opportunities that align with my values and passions.

I have the power to turn my dreams into financial success.

Every financial decision I make is leading me toward more abundance.

I surround myself with positive influences that encourage wealth creation.

I attract high-paying opportunities that match my skills and worth.

Money is always circulating and returning to me multiplied.

I have an abundance mindset that attracts prosperity in every area of my life.

I honor my financial goals by taking action daily.

I am deeply connected to the wealth and prosperity of my ancestors.

I am financially independent and enjoy the freedom it brings.

I use my money to create joy, impact, and lasting success.

My wealth grows as I share my gifts with the world.

I am empowered to make decisions that grow my financial wealth.

I embrace a life filled with luxury, wealth, and comfort.

My success is inevitable, and my financial future is secure.

I am in control of my finances and make wise choices with my money.

I always find new and creative ways to build wealth.

I align my financial goals with my highest purpose.

I attract people and opportunities that increase my financial success.

I celebrate my financial achievements and set new wealth goals.

I attract limitless abundance and prosperity into my life.

I have the mindset of a wealthy, successful Black woman.

My financial future is secure because I take inspired action.

I make investments that multiply my wealth and increase my security.

I welcome financial blessings from expected and unexpected sources.

I am a magnet for financial growth, stability, and opportunity.

I use money wisely to create the life I deserve.

My thoughts are focused on financial expansion and limitless success.

I respect and manage my money with wisdom and care.

I turn every challenge into an opportunity for financial success.

I am a walking embodiment of abundance, prosperity, and wealth.

I bless others with my wealth, and it returns to me tenfold.

My financial success is inspiring others to claim their own abundance.

I embrace money as a positive force in my life.

I set clear financial goals and achieve them with ease.

My financial dreams are becoming reality each day.

I honor my worth by expecting and accepting financial abundance.

The more I give, the more I receive — my wealth is limitless.

I am grateful for the financial opportunities that come my way.

I am successful because I believe in myself and my abilities.

My confidence attracts prosperity and financial success.

I take full responsibility for my financial success and abundance.

Every action I take moves me closer to financial independence.

I am proud of my financial growth and discipline.

I embody the energy of success, wealth, and abundance.

I am grateful for the resources that contribute to my financial prosperity.

I welcome massive financial breakthroughs into my life.

My life is overflowing with abundance in every way.

I am a Black woman building generational wealth, and I claim my financial freedom.

Part 2: Attracting Opportunities and Financial Freedom

Opportunities flow to me effortlessly and abundantly.

I attract wealth and success with ease.

Financial freedom is my birthright, and I claim it boldly.

I am a magnet for life-changing opportunities.

Money flows to me in expected and unexpected ways.

I welcome prosperity into my life with open arms.

My skills, talents, and passions attract financial success.

The universe is constantly opening doors of abundance for me.

Every day, I attract new opportunities that align with my purpose.

I am financially independent and secure.

I am open to receiving all the wealth that is meant for me.

I create wealth through my gifts and hard work.

My mind is a powerful tool for manifesting abundance.

I attract people and opportunities that support my financial growth.

My potential for success is limitless.

I am worthy of wealth and financial success.

I see opportunities where others see obstacles.

I trust the journey and know that financial freedom is mine.

Money is an unlimited resource, and I have access to it at all times.

My wealth expands every day, in every way.

I welcome unexpected blessings and financial breakthroughs.

The work I do today leads to my future abundance.

I am grateful for all the opportunities that come my way.

Every challenge I overcome brings me closer to financial freedom.

I take inspired action to achieve financial independence.

I am financially free, and my life is abundant.

My bank account is constantly growing.

I am the architect of my financial destiny.

I make smart, strategic decisions that build long-term wealth.

My income is increasing every day.

I align myself with people who inspire and motivate me to succeed.

I attract mentors and guides who help me grow financially.

Wealth is attracted to me because I am in alignment with prosperity.

My financial success benefits not only me but also my family and community.

I attract opportunities that elevate my financial status.

I am constantly being rewarded for my hard work and dedication.

My financial goals are achievable and within my reach.

I am confident in my ability to create and manage wealth.

I attract high-value opportunities that change my life for the better.

I am creating a legacy of abundance for generations to come.

I am financially intelligent and make wise investments.

I deserve to live a life free from financial stress.

My income streams multiply effortlessly.

I am grateful for the financial blessings that come into my life.

I welcome prosperity with open arms and an open heart.

Every step I take brings me closer to my financial goals.

I am a wealth builder and a financial trailblazer.

I am unstoppable when it comes to achieving financial success.

My vision is clear, and I pursue it fearlessly.

I manifest financial stability, wealth, and freedom with ease.

My money mindset is strong, abundant, and limitless.

I release all fears surrounding money and replace them with confidence.

I am aligned with wealth, prosperity, and endless opportunities.

I trust that financial abundance is always available to me.

I am a magnet for success and financial prosperity.

I make wise decisions that create long-term financial success.

I am worthy of earning and receiving large sums of money.

I release limiting beliefs about money and step into financial freedom.

My bank account reflects the abundance I attract into my life.

I attract lucrative opportunities that expand my income.

I am fearless in my pursuit of financial success.

I create wealth while making a positive impact in the world.

I align my actions with the wealth I desire.

I am constantly upgrading my financial mindset.

I make smart financial decisions that lead to lasting abundance.

Every day, I expand my capacity for receiving wealth.

My life is filled with endless opportunities to prosper.

I am grateful for the financial blessings that continue to come my way.

I confidently make choices that lead to financial stability and wealth.

I allow money to flow into my life with ease.

I am always in the right place at the right time for financial opportunities.

I deserve a life of abundance, wealth, and financial security.

My financial future is bright, and I welcome it with joy.

The universe always provides me with exactly what I need.

I trust that all my financial needs are being met.

My hard work and dedication are constantly rewarded.

I attract wealth through creativity, determination, and faith.

I release all financial worries and embrace security.

I make money easily and frequently.

I am constantly leveling up my financial mindset.

My thoughts, actions, and energy align with financial prosperity.

I am intentional with my finances and attract stability.

My income continues to grow as I expand my skills and knowledge.

I am open to new sources of income and financial growth.

Wealth and success flow to me in abundance.

I am building multiple streams of income with ease.

I am always attracting opportunities that support my financial goals.

I welcome wealth into my life without hesitation.

Every action I take moves me toward financial freedom.

My financial goals are already manifesting in my life.

I trust my ability to attract wealth and success.

My prosperity benefits everyone around me.

I embrace financial abundance with gratitude and joy.

My mindset is programmed for success and financial stability.

I am always expanding my ability to earn and receive money.

My work is valuable, and I am compensated accordingly.

I am fearless in making financial decisions that benefit me.

I expect financial miracles and blessings every day.

My path is clear, and my success is inevitable.

I am a powerful creator of wealth, success, and abundance.

Part 3: Overcoming Imposter Syndrome

I belong in every space I enter.

My voice is powerful, and my words have impact.

I am more than qualified for every opportunity that comes my way.

I do not need permission to be great—I already am.

I trust myself and my abilities fully.

My success is not luck; it is the result of my hard work and talent.

I do not compare my journey to anyone else's — my path is unique.

I release all doubts about my skills and expertise.

I deserve every achievement I have earned.

My presence is valuable, and I bring something special to the table.

I am a force to be reckoned with.

I reject the lies that tell me I am not enough.

I have the experience, knowledge, and talent to succeed.

I have earned my place, and I claim it with confidence.

I am more than capable of handling challenges that come my way.

I let go of fear and embrace my success with open arms.

My work speaks for itself, and I stand by my accomplishments.

I will not let self-doubt silence my brilliance.

I am intelligent, capable, and worthy of every opportunity I receive.

I refuse to let fear keep me from stepping into my power.

I honor my achievements and celebrate my growth.

I have worked hard to be where I am, and I am proud of myself.

I am not an imposter — I am an innovator.

I trust that I am exactly where I am meant to be.

I allow myself to feel proud of all I have accomplished.

I am confident in my skills and expertise.

I do not need external validation — I know my worth.

I am enough just as I am.

My value is not measured by anyone else's opinion.

I release all feelings of self-doubt and embrace my greatness.

I have everything I need within me to succeed.

I am not afraid to take up space and shine.

I bring unique perspectives and talents that deserve to be seen.

I let go of limiting beliefs and embrace my capabilities.

I do not let setbacks define me — I keep pushing forward.

I am more than worthy of my success.

I do not need to have all the answers — I am always learning and growing.

I choose confidence over fear every single day.

I acknowledge my strengths and trust in my ability to thrive.

I do not allow self-doubt to rob me of my joy.

My skills and talents make a difference in the world.

I trust my intuition and inner wisdom.

I bring value to every conversation, project, and opportunity.

I deserve to be seen, heard, and respected.

I embrace my expertise and step into leadership with confidence.

I will not apologize for my success — I have earned it.

I have the power to create the life and career I desire.

I am not afraid to ask for what I deserve.

I no longer question whether I belong — I know I do.

I take ownership of my accomplishments and stand tall in them.

I celebrate myself and my achievements every day.

I am a Black woman, and I am limitless.

I am not defined by my fears—I am defined by my resilience.

My presence alone is powerful and meaningful.

I am a valuable contributor, and my work speaks for itself.

I will not shrink myself to make others comfortable.

I am bold, confident, and unstoppable.

I release all doubts and step fully into my potential.

I embrace my worth and walk in my greatness.

My achievements are well-earned, and I am proud of them.

I let go of perfectionism and embrace progress.

My unique perspective is needed and valuable.

I do not need to prove my worth — I already know it.

I choose to believe in myself, even when it's hard.

I am more than my insecurities — I am my strengths and successes.

I belong in spaces of influence, power, and success.

My presence is not an accident—I am here for a reason.

I am fearless in the face of challenges.

I give myself credit for my hard work and dedication.

I am worthy of recognition, success, and celebration.

I trust in my abilities to continue learning and growing.

I will not let imposter syndrome hold me back from greatness.

I embrace my full potential with confidence and grace.

I release any fear of failure and embrace new opportunities.

My success is a reflection of my skills and determination.

I do not need to over-explain my worth—I embody it.

I have earned the right to stand in my power.

I believe in my vision and trust in my path.

My energy is magnetic, and I attract success effortlessly.

I give myself permission to thrive.

I honor the work I have put in to get where I am today.

My story is still unfolding, and it is filled with success.

I am equipped for every opportunity that comes my way.

I do not let fear stop me from pursuing my dreams.

I am fearless, bold, and driven.

I am proud of my uniqueness and the impact I make.

I trust that I am on the right path.

My knowledge, experience, and voice are valuable.

I am worthy of every accolade, recognition, and opportunity.

I walk in confidence, knowing I am capable of great things.

I no longer let fear dictate my actions.

My hard work, effort, and dedication have brought me here.

I am stepping into my power without hesitation.

I deserve to be in spaces of leadership and influence.

I am worthy of mentorship, guidance, and opportunities for growth.

I am not afraid to advocate for myself and my success.

I radiate confidence, intelligence, and ambition.

I am capable of breaking barriers and shattering ceilings.

I embrace challenges as stepping stones to my success.

I am proud of who I am, what I have accomplished, and where I am headed.

Part 4: Staying Focused on Goals

I am committed to my goals and take steps toward them every day.

My vision is clear, and I pursue it with focus and passion.

Distractions do not control me — I remain laser-focused.

I am disciplined, determined, and dedicated to my success.

I trust in my ability to stay on track and achieve greatness.

My goals are worth my time and effort.

I wake up every day with purpose and drive.

My success is built on my consistency and dedication.

I choose to focus on progress, not perfection.

I embrace challenges as opportunities to grow stronger.

I release all excuses and take full responsibility for my progress.

I am in control of my thoughts, my time, and my actions.

I do not let fear, doubt, or negativity distract me.

Every setback is a setup for a stronger comeback.

I rise above distractions and stay focused on what truly matters.

My energy flows where my focus goes—I focus on my success.

I am bigger than my obstacles and stronger than my fears.

I release procrastination and embrace action.

I learn from challenges and use them to fuel my determination.

I do not give up—I adjust my approach and keep going.

I use my time wisely, investing in things that move me forward.

I set clear priorities and stick to them.

Every task I complete brings me one step closer to my dreams.

I am productive, efficient, and intentional with my time.

I create and follow a plan for success.

My time is valuable, and I protect it fiercely.

I break big goals into small, achievable steps.

I embrace structure and routine to stay on track.

I eliminate distractions and focus on meaningful work.

I honor my commitments to myself and my future.

I believe in myself and my ability to succeed.

I have everything I need within me to reach my goals.

My dreams are valid, and I work toward them with confidence.

I deserve success, and I work hard for it.

I step into my power, knowing I am capable of achieving greatness.

I trust that my hard work will pay off.

My goals are important, and I give them my full attention.

I stay motivated, even when the journey gets tough.

I am resilient, and I refuse to quit.

My passion fuels my drive, and my drive fuels my success.

I take consistent action toward my goals every day.

Each step forward builds momentum toward my success.

I celebrate my progress and stay motivated.

I am patient with my journey while remaining persistent.

I push through challenges because I know my success is inevitable.

I create my future with every action I take today.

I stay inspired and remind myself why I started.

I am excited about my growth and my potential.

My motivation comes from within—I do not rely on external validation.

I keep my eyes on my vision, no matter what comes my way.

I do not allow fear to hold me back.

My confidence grows stronger with every goal I accomplish.

I silence self-doubt with action and self-belief.

I am worthy of all the success coming my way.

I trust my journey, even when the path is unclear.

I do not compare myself to others — I focus on my progress.

My abilities are limitless, and I step into my greatness.

I let go of perfectionism and embrace continuous improvement.

My success story is unfolding exactly as it should.

I choose courage over comfort every day.

I am unstoppable in the pursuit of my dreams.

My mindset is strong, and I do not waver in my determination.

I bounce back from setbacks stronger than before.

I trust the process and keep moving forward.

I turn obstacles into stepping stones toward my goals.

I am built for success, and nothing can break my spirit.

My resilience is my superpower, and I use it wisely.

I overcome challenges with grace and strength.

I do not allow temporary struggles to define my journey.

I am more powerful than any challenge that comes my way.

I see myself achieving my goals, and I make it happen.

I visualize my success and attract it into my reality.

I align my thoughts and actions with success.

I am creating the future I desire through my focused efforts.

I manifest opportunities and success through my mindset.

My dreams are becoming reality because I take action.

I trust that the universe is aligning everything for my highest good.

I stay positive and expect great things to happen.

I speak life into my goals, knowing they are within reach.

My faith in my journey keeps me motivated every day.

I remain committed to my vision, no matter what.

My discipline leads to my success.

I hold myself accountable for my growth.

I do not make excuses — I take action.

My future self will thank me for the work I put in today.

I do not let comfort zones keep me from my full potential.

I stay focused because my goals matter.

I am patient, knowing that success takes time and effort.

I am dedicated to my dreams and work for them daily.

I remain consistent because I know consistency leads to results.

I enjoy the process of achieving my goals.

Every step forward is a victory, no matter how small.

I celebrate my wins and use them as motivation.

I learn from every challenge and grow stronger.

I am grateful for my progress and excited for my future.

My growth journey is beautiful, and I embrace every moment.

I remain flexible and open to new opportunities.

My purpose fuels my passion, and my passion fuels my success.

I trust that I am on the right path, even when it takes unexpected turns.

I am focused, unstoppable, and destined for greatness.

Part 5: Entrepreneurial Success Affirmations

I am a successful and confident entrepreneur.

My ideas are valuable, and I trust in my vision.

I am fully capable of building a thriving business.

I step into my entrepreneurial journey with boldness and faith.

I deserve to be successful, and I claim my success with confidence.

I am an expert in my field, and my skills create value.

My business is a reflection of my creativity and brilliance.

I do not fear competition — my uniqueness sets me apart.

I trust myself to make smart, strategic business decisions.

I am worthy of financial success and the life of my dreams.

Money flows to me easily through my business.

I attract abundance and financial prosperity effortlessly.

My business generates wealth that supports my ideal lifestyle.

I am building generational wealth through my work.

I am grateful for every financial blessing that comes my way.

My revenue increases daily, and I am prepared to receive more.

I am open to receiving limitless financial opportunities.

My business is a magnet for success and abundance.

I make money doing what I love, and I love making money.

Every sale, client, and opportunity brings me closer to my financial goals.

I am resilient, and no challenge can break me.

I face setbacks with courage, knowing they are stepping stones to growth.

My failures are lessons that lead to greater success.

I do not let fear stop me from pursuing my dreams.

Every obstacle is an opportunity for innovation and expansion.

I am flexible and adapt to any changes in my industry.

I am a problem solver, and I always find solutions.

My perseverance will lead me to incredible achievements.

I release self-doubt and trust the process.

I turn every "no" into motivation for a greater "yes."

My business attracts the right clients with ease.

I provide exceptional value, and my clients recognize it.

I am building a loyal customer base that trusts and supports my brand.

Opportunities flow to me in expected and unexpected ways.

I am highly sought after because of my talent and expertise.

My brand is strong, and people are excited to work with me.

I attract business collaborations that align with my vision.

My reputation precedes me — I am known for excellence.

I confidently share my products and services because they are impactful.

I build meaningful connections that propel my business forward.

I wake up every day excited to grow my business.

I manage my time effectively and stay focused on my goals.

I am disciplined, determined, and dedicated to my success.

Every action I take moves my business in the right direction.

I prioritize tasks that lead to the biggest results.

I am organized, strategic, and intentional in my work.

My consistency ensures my long-term success.

I work efficiently and maximize my productivity daily.

I balance my work and personal life with grace and ease.

I am the CEO of my life, and I run it with confidence.

My brand is powerful, and I market it with pride.

I confidently promote my business because I believe in its value.

My message resonates with the right audience.

I use my voice to inspire and attract opportunities.

My business is seen, heard, and respected in my industry.

I am a thought leader, and people listen when I speak.

I share my story with confidence, knowing it inspires others.

My online presence attracts abundance and opportunities.

I am worthy of press, publicity, and recognition for my work.

I am confident in charging what I'm worth because I provide value.

My business is growing beyond my wildest dreams.

I am expanding into new markets and opportunities effortlessly.

I attract investors, partners, and clients who believe in my vision.

My team and support system help me scale my business successfully.

I make strategic decisions that grow my brand sustainably.

I invest in myself and my business, knowing it leads to long-term success.

My business is a force for good, making a meaningful impact.

I am a powerhouse entrepreneur with limitless potential.

I attract mentors and coaches who guide me to greatness.

I confidently step into the next level of my success.

My work is valuable, and I price it accordingly.

I do not undervalue myself — my time and expertise are priceless.

I confidently ask for and receive what I am worth.

My clients happily invest in my services because they see the results.

I charge premium prices because my work is premium quality.

Money is energy, and I attract high-value opportunities.

I do not negotiate my worth — I stand firm in my pricing.

My wealth grows as I confidently position myself in the market.

I believe in the value I bring to the world.

I attract high-paying clients who appreciate and respect my work.

I am building a legacy that will impact generations to come.

I trust that every step I take leads to greater success.

I am committed to lifelong learning and continuous improvement.

I am always evolving and embracing new opportunities for success.

My business is sustainable, profitable, and fulfilling.

I celebrate every milestone, no matter how big or small.

I deserve joy, abundance, and prosperity in my entrepreneurial journey.

I am financially free and empowered through my business.

My dreams are valid, and I will never stop pursuing them.

I remain humble and grateful as my business flourishes.

My success paves the way for other Black women to rise.

I uplift and support other Black women in business.

I use my platform to inspire and educate those around me.

I give back to my community in meaningful ways.

My business serves a greater purpose beyond profit.

I am a role model, showing others what's possible.

I mentor, teach, and empower the next generation of Black entrepreneurs.

I am making history with every move I make.

I embody abundance, confidence, and excellence.

I was born to lead, build, and create wealth—I own my power.

Thank You!

Hello Beautiful Soul,

I truly hope you have enjoyed this book and that these affirmations have uplifted, empowered, and reminded you of the strength and beauty within you. Your journey to self-love and confidence is powerful, and I am honored to be a part of it.

If this book has inspired you, I would love to hear your thoughts. Many readers don't realize how much reviews mean to authors like me—they help spread the word so that more women can benefit from these affirmations. Your review doesn't have to be long; just a few words sharing your experience can make a big difference.

If you'd like to support this book and help others discover it, please take a moment to leave a review by clicking the link below or scanning the QR code with your phone. Your support means the world to me, and I am deeply grateful for it.

Thank you for being here. Thank you for showing up for yourself. Thank you for allowing me to be a small part of your journey.

With love and gratitude,

Tamara Jackson

www.ingramcontent.com/pod-product-compliance
Lightning Source LLC
Chambersburg PA
CBHW070154080526
44586CB00015B/1980